# Death, Please Wait

Poems

Available from Small Press Distribution and Amazon, also from Box Turtle Press, Inc.
184 Franklin Street
New York, New York 10013
212.219.9278; mudfishmag@aol.com
www.mudfish.org

ISBN: 978-1-893654-32-7

Cover: Jill Hoffman, "The Psychics's Wedding," detail, 2023. Oil on Canvas, 30"x36"
Book Design: Anne Lawrence
Typeset in Futura Book


Publisher: Box Turtle Press, Inc.
Box Turtle Press, Inc. is a 501(c)(3) not-for-profit organization.

MUDFISH INDIVIDUAL POET SERIES #19

# Death, Please Wait

## Poems

Rochelle Jewel Shapiro

Box Turtle Press
184 Franklin Street, New York, New York 10013

ALSO BY ROCHELLE JEWEL SHAPIRO:

**Novel**

*Miriam the Medium* (Simon & Schuster, 2005)

For my husband, Bernie (1944-2022)
and our children,
children's children,
and all who are healing from loss

*"Bereavement is not the truncation of a married life, but one of its regular phases like the honeymoon. "*

C.S. Lewis

# TABLE OF CONTENTS

TABLE OF CONTENTS continued | PAGE

PAGE

# WHEN DID IT START

When he sideswiped the car on the garage weatherstripping, the first time?
The third?
When, with blizzard warnings, he wanted to drive to the Botanical Gardens,
and stood jangling the car keys in his pocket even as hail began to ping
against our windows?
When he went to PayLess and bought eleven pairs of shoes?
When he began riding his stationary bike throughout the night, the creaking
    and clacking like dungeon sounds?
When he bought twenty thin plastic bags of unlabeled oatmeal, as if we were
    preparing to start an Oliver Twist orphanage? When he stored the oat
    meal on the top shelf of our walk-in closet along with the knife sets and
    Tupperware he'd bought?
When I walked into that closet and the bags of oatmeal fell over, ripping
open, strewing me with oatmeal like a bride whose guests ran out of
rice, shouldn't I have known that something was wrong?

# AT FOURTEEN

To have fallen in love when you are only a year
older than Juliette and your beloved only a year
older than Romeo, you can't stop drawing Bic-
pen hearts in the margins of your black
and white marbleized notebooks or carving
them into your school desk or drawing them on
your breath in the school bus window.

Nights, you clutch your pillow
to your chest and whisper his name
into your pillowcase. Your skin
holds heat, even in winter.

In your pink vinyl diary with the pony-tailed girl
wearing a long white button-down shirt and black
clamdiggers on the cover, you write in Spanish
to keep your secrets from your mother—

*T'amo Bernardo*
*Bernardo y yo siempre*
*Bernardo y yo besando mucho*

O when he whispers, "I love you,"
you can hear and feel the words in
your ear even when you're apart
the way a seashell holds the sea,
the way you can hear him now.

# SPRAYED ROSES

I set the roses in a cut
glass vase of water,
added powder from the
packet every Valentine's
Day to make them last
beyond the death of roses
when all I wanted
was you,

but you are not lasting. I
will never again feel
the heat of you as you
hand me a bouquet, never
again float entwined
with you.

# MAY I ASK YOUR NAME

You were seventeen when you knelt
at my beach blanket. Faltering,
reddening, you said, *I'm Bernie.*
*May I ask your name?*

Named for your uncle who they thought was dead
but was located in an Amsterdam hospital in a full
body cast two years after the war,

you wore your uncle's story like barbed wire.
It impelled you to wake at four a.m. as if for roll-
call, *Appellplatz*, and drive in blizzards, in
hurricanes, the twenty miles to your pharmacy where
pills dropped into the pill counter like a hail of
bullets, where the paperwork was chipping boulders
with a tiny pickaxe.

Now, in bed, your eyes dart around the
hospital room. Delirious after open heart
surgery, you say, *He's here, Mengeles,*
*the Angel of Death.* Your long body
thrashes, trying to get up, straining the IV
lines and catheters.

*I'll find a way for us to escape*, you whisper, but
*if I can't, then you go on without me.*

Now I must.

# MAKING OUR WAY AMONG THE SHADOWS

I believed you, my husband, 6′4″ and fierce-eyed, would be
like Aeneus who survived the sacking of Troy, and I, like his
wife, Creusa, would someday be a ghost you called out to,
reached for, but could no longer touch. You, who I watched,
heart-pounding, wrestle a knife-wielding mugger to the gum-
splotched sidewalk, you, who walked home miles and miles
in the black of the NYC blackout, stopping to direct cars with
your pocket flashlight, you, who were robbed in your
pharmacy five times at gunpoint, once with the gun held
to your temple as you tried to explain that the drugs they
wanted were already stolen that week, you who went to the
projects run by the Crips and the Bloods to deliver diabetic
supplies to your customers, you who fought off pneumonia
three times without missing work, would go on long after me.

But in the end, my warrior, it was you
who left me reaching for you, calling
"Bernie, Bernie, Bernie."

# MAN OF MOONLIGHT

On the horizon of sleep, you walk toward me on strong legs,
get into our bed, not the railed one at the nursing home.
You rock me in your long arms like the boat moored
on the black river that I will board and row to you.

What song will I sing to convince
the gods to free you? I will dare to pass my dead father
and his ready fists and the other shades who lurk
and moan on the shores of the Styx. I will dare
to near Cerberus to get to you, the fierce three-headed dog,
though I'm terrified of unleashed dogs
from my father's stories
of the Cossacks' hounds that hunted
for Jews in the forest.

My vocal cords will keen, ululate, toll
a song that opens the hearts of your captors.
They will allow you to walk again and follow me
out the electric doors into the parking lot
crowded with the cars of aides, nurses, and doctors.

I will walk a few steps before you, then look
over my shoulder, watch your soul lift
from your bone-thin, ashen body, your ulcerated foot,
your breath that comes in groaning gulps.

You will return to me each night, glowing,

made of moonbeams, and neither of us
will ever again have to see
that cribbed bed from hell.

# LANDING

Those nights we lay on the beach blanket
looking up at the moon, your leg thrown over
my hip, the salt air licking our skin, we felt
the lift-off of a flying dream.

Now I'm suited-up, my face masked and visored,
my body robed in blue, my hands in blue Latex
gloves. You blink and blink at me.
Can you tell I'm your wife?
COVID has quarantined your wing of the nursing home, ten
residents down, how many more to go?

I wonder if you remember when we watched Aldrin and Armstrong
lowering their suited bodies, lumbering and bounding,
heard their scratchy voices? When they planted the flag,
you kissed me hard on the mouth.

Gravity has brought us to this: you,
bedridden, pale, limbs thinned and
crooked from disuse and me,
sweltering in plastic, my forehead
squeezed by the vise of the face
shield, my sheathed hands unable to
touch your skin, and you with your
glazed eyes.

# ON THE EDGE OF SLEEP

I am at the edge of the bed where you and I slept.
I can't bear to stretch, to claim the side you
staked out, and the middle where we spooned is
not yet where I can put myself.

The bed is a country, a landscape of soft snores
and deep sighs. Widowed is still wedded. Bed
no longer has a translation in the burst of
bombs for all the widows of Ukraine.

On the edge of sleep, I think of the orphans
crossing borders alone, dragging their blankets
and stuffed bears. If Ukraine is ever free again,
where will mourners lay their flowers? Where
will they kneel to whisper, "I miss you?"

Mornings, I bless each mouthful of breakfast,
the sky for its quiet blue, only shattered by
the cawing of crows that the town wants to
chase out with laser lights.

In rain, in snow, beneath the bluest of skies, your relatives
were known by the blue numbers tattooed on their forearms,
were pushed into mass graves, body stacked on body. Or
burned in ovens, their ashes filling the sky with plumes of
stench and darkness.

The nursing home staff knows you as Bernie in 328
who needs to be changed, turned, and fed
as snow falls
in this, the winter of our lives.

# MURMUR

*Rochelle,* you whisper. I feel your breath in
my ear. I open my eyes, blink at your side
of the bed that's empty of you.

You, a stomach-sleeper, your profile still
impressed in the down pillow, your blue
waffle-weave blanket rumpled, but flat
without cocooning you.

I remember you told me of your early morning
cardiologist appointment. With my head on
your chest, I've listened to the whump,
whump of your aortic murmur.

How, I wonder, did I feel your breath,
and hear your voice vibrate though the air
in waves like the rush of the sea at the
beach where we first met?

I microwave the half-cup of coffee you
left over. It warms my lips.

# HOSPITAL CURTAIN

Your eyes are huge above your face mask.
You, my husband, wince as I drop you off
at the emergency room. I must leave you
in the latex-gloved hands of strangers.

This morning, I woke to you curled beside me,
moaning softly, your knees almost beneath your chin.
            *I didn't want to wake you*, you said.
We sprang up, dressed. Now I pace the living room
talking to you, three miles away.

You, stalwart as your uncle who survived Auschwitz,
tell me calmly what the MRI and Cat Scan show. I
hear the *shhh* and clatter of the hospital curtain, then
the rumble of you being transported.

You never ended the call.
I stayed on the phone, listening.

# ONCE

When gulls flapped madly in the darkening sky
and the wind became razors,
my mother-in-law looked out her fourth-floor window
to watch the hurricane hit. What she saw
was you, my husband, at seven,
            holding your five-year-old brother's hand, leading
him toward the beach to see
            what the sky and roiling
sea had in store. My mother-in-law
            ran, screaming
                        your names, dragged you both home
by your ears for a scolding
that rattled you and your brother
                        like the wind beating the windows.

You should have left the beach with me
            when the wind whipped up. "Let's go," I yelled,
but you stood your ground
in the sand as if to test your mettle. The wind
whooshed. I felt my feet lift.
            You grabbed my hands,
                        held on so the wind wouldn't take me
                        without you.
As quick as the squall came, it left.
                        We faced each other, breathless, laughing.

The next day, I would not have believed it

except for your bruising fingerprints on my hands,
my hands too tender to do anything
but rest in my pockets. I knew, no matter what
                    danger you drew me into, you
                    would never let go of me.

# I LOVE YOU LIKE GERMAN BLACK FOREST CAKE

The ooze of whipped cream
and spongy Schokolade, the squish
of pitted cherries with their gleam,
foam lapping like a wave in a Hokusai
woodcut that comes alive, *Ich liebe.*

O, the deliciousness of lying entwined with you
on the moist bottom of the Black Forest, light
shafting between the silver firs, striping us like
prisoners of this aphrodisiac spiked
with *kirschwasser.*

Just saying the throaty name,
*Schwarzwälder Kirschtorte,* makes
me coo
*Mein mann, ich liebe dich.* Like a
German Black Forest Cake,
I love you.

# JOHNNY MATHIS CONCERT, 1962

Holding hands, thighs pressed together, we leaned forward in our tier at Arthur Ashe Stadium where Johnny Mathis was to be raised from a below-the-stage platform. His voice floated up like aged bourbon, warming us. His head appeared from the neck up, but the platform got stuck. We watched for long moments as his head sang *Star eyes, flashing eyes in which my hopes rise* until stagehands figured out how to elevate him.

After that, we could never make out to his records without bursting into laughter.

His lyrics were cornball, but they comfort me now.

*I need you O, my darling, like the roses need rain.*

*Until the 12th of never, I'll still be loving you.*

# WEDDING ALBUM, 1967

Oh, here's my mother in pink chiffon and a Jackie Kennedy pillbox hat,
her hand on mine as if she hadn't just snarled,
*You're a rotten daughter, rotten.*

Now I'm pinning a boutonnière on my father's lapel
while he mutters beneath a pasted-on grin,
*We needed flowers for men, yet?*

On this page my parents are together until death did them part.
*You'll be the death of me,* she always told him.
*You'll live to dance on my grave,* he'd shoot back.

Those tables of guests, the dance
floor of fox-trotters, most
of them dead now.

The last page is you and I
silhouetted in a near-kiss. You,
trussed in a cummerbund beneath your black tails,
me, cinch-waisted, barely able to take a quarter-breath.

We should have floated toward each other
in ultramarine air like Chagall's lovers, me in your arms
holding a bouquet of wildflowers.

# MARCEL PROUST

In Swann's Way, a bite of a Madelaine evoked memory.
For me, it was a tuna sandwich made on one slice of toast
to save calories. When I brought it to my mouth, the tuna
glopped through the toast and fell, clump by clump,
sopping my fingers, plate, table, and lap.

I remembered the stranger who stopped me on
Central Avenue a few months after we married.
"Hey, aren't you Bernie's wife?" he asked.

"How did you know?"

"Me and a couple of other guys take the A train with him. He
showed us your picture. Whoa, is that guy in love,
but let me give you a tip. Stop making those tuna sandwiches.
They soak through the bag, and he has to wrap the mess
up in the newspaper he was looking forward to reading."

"Why didn't you tell me about the mess the tuna sandwiches were
making?" I asked him that night.

"It was so nice of you to make them for me," he said.
"I didn't want to hurt your feelings."

# SHELBOURNE CHEMISTS, INC., 1973

On 18th Avenue, when the sky over Brooklyn still bears traces of night and garbage is bedewed with midnight drizzle, the dark men from the Egyptian luncheonette share smoke from a hookah. Beneath shrill laughter and Arabic, the gypsy's chicken *buk, buks* through an open window.

We unlock the padlock,
slide the security gate aside, walk through the metal door, dip to turn off the alarm, rise to switch on the bars of buzzing florescent lights that expose the smile-like heel smudges on the blue and white tile floor of the pharmacy that is your kingdom.

Soon pills hail down into the pill counter tray. The *tat tat tat* of labels being typed. Those labels, affixed to the transparent brown vials, bearing names of the living, are filled with pills to keep the living alive, the poor and the old and the immigrants who come in with rich breaths of paprika, jerk seasoning, cumin, garlic, chipotle pepper, and kasha.

# BITTERSWEET

The stiffening of your lips, your white-knuckled-
wheel-grip, darting eyes, signal that a car is trying
to cut into your lane. Your driving makes
passengers' hands fly to the sides of their faces,
their jaws go slack, their eyes pop, like in
Edvard Munch's *The Scream*.

The fifty-three years of our marriage tarred
with *I'm sorry* and promises that never stick.
Your rage is fired-up like a pot in a kiln.
So many of your relatives were herded off
to Camps, helpless. Ash.
You feel you must fight back. You must.

"When will Europe be over?" our
daughter used to ask.

"We're safe," I remind you, touching your
shoulder. You slow down, wave on the other car.
As if the strangling bittersweet and garlic mustard
vines were cleared from the roadside trees,
I feel light seep back in.

# YANKEE GAME IN 100 DEGREES

My husband takes a grinning bite of
his Nathan's hot dog.
When we got married, his mother threw
away all his baseball cards.
Sweat scalds my eyeballs.
There are rows of empty seats.
Aaron Judge is back from his back injury.
Damp palms clap for him.
Pigeons flap across the field.
Clouds canoodle in their bed of blue.
Aaron Hicks makes a deep hit to right field.
Aaron Judge runs from second to third. Didi
Gregorius slides head-first, stomach down, arms
outstretched, onto the base the way I, as a child,
rode the waves at Rockaway Beach.
I'm at this game because I love him.

# LOT

Only one of your hearing aids works.
Me, muzzy-sighted. You, half deaf.
I said: Let me hold the remote. I can hear
the *blat blat blat* of our car alarm.
You said: No, I can find our car. Trust me.
That was an hour ago.
Heat pours on my head like cooked honey.
The nerve in my big right toe sizzles.
Gulls circle the roof of Target.
A young mother pushing her daughter in a stroller
smirks at me. *I was her once. She will be me.*
Someone's remote sets off an alarm.
Our silver Hyundai lights up, bleats.
Yes, my umbrella's inside next to your hat,
but I'm locked out. You are somewhere,
walking with that remote, pointing it here, there,
as if it were a divining rod. Will our battery go?
Where are you? I wave my arms in the air.
Slowly, a tall smudge, you come toward me.
You open the door. I want to beat my fists
against your shoulder. We're on our wordless way,
a hissy fit of wind against my window. You grip
the steering wheel with one hand,
the other fisted on your thigh.

# WHEN NO ONE IS NEAR US

When no one is near us, we take off our masks.
My husband, a boy again, skips shells.
I gather translucent jingle shells, slipper shells,

blue-black mussels, fluted scallops, pale purple-brown moon
snails, whorled whelks, opalescent oyster shells, carry them
in the makeshift basket of my skirt.

Walking back, I feel the grass flatten beneath
my soles and tuft between my toes.
Cotton whites and monarchs

light on daylilies, astilbe, coneflowers, phlox, black-eyed
Susans, lantanas, and blazing stars.
I lean in to smell the flowers.

My husband, laughing, takes my picture.
My nose is yellow with pollen.
Will we have to shelter-in again?

# HIS LEATHER JACKET

When he moves, the loam-
colored leather rustles like
leaf fall. The stitches,
thread bumps, hillocks,
the collar creased at his
nape, the grain like dry
riverbeds, cuffs and
waistband, a stretchy knit,
a bit scratchy like his
unshaven chin. His pocket
can swallow my hand.
The zipper, toothed as a
too-hard kiss. I love to grip
the epaulets, trace my
finger along the crinkly
seams, breathe in the
leather that holds his scent.

# MARRIAGE

I watch you grow more ashen.
You barely eat.
"I'm fine," you insist.

I wake up in a sweat, put my ear
to the lips I've kissed for years.
You breathe. If you died of
stubbornness, how could I
grieve?

By Saturday, hands and legs
trembling, you finally agree to
go to the walk-in clinic.

The doc says it's pneumonia.

If you die, my hair will turn to hay,
my skin a carapace. I'll heave
tempest sighs that shudder the
earth, my tongue will forever
stutter your name.

# MEDIEVAL HERB GARDEN

"Sweet sweet sweet tow-ee," my husband trills
to the sparrow on a branch, and it calls back. He
bends, knees cracking, to smell the bitter scent
of the rue's greenish-yellow blooms.

"The juice of rue will guard you against the
biting of serpents," he reads from the plaque,
"also the stinging of scorpions, spiders,
bees, hornets, and wasps."

The sky is pale blue, yet I fear the air is full
of hobgoblins jealous of our marriage. I
squeeze rue blossoms between my fingers,
press the juice onto our lips, our tongues.

# HER GHOST

I knew she was haunting you. You'd be sitting on the
couch, the velveteen one sewn with plastic thread that
snapped here and there, sticking up like a bed of nails,
you'd cock your head, your newspaper dropping
to your lap, jaw slack, eyes blinking and blinking,

or when you'd cry out in your sleep, "Don't, don't do it,"
and I'd rub your back and whisper, "It wasn't your fault,
it wasn't."

It started the night you got an alert from the alarm
company that your pharmacy was on fire, and you
drove the twenty miles, foot heavy on the gas. You
phoned to say the fire took place in one of the
apartments above the store. That night, and the
next, you slept in a sleeping bag on the floor of
your pharmacy to let repairmen in, and still you
filled prescriptions all day.

The fire had been set, the fire marshal told you,
by a little girl left alone, lighting matches.

You were there when the mother came home that night
and shrieked at finding her daughter had been taken
into foster care. You were there that night, asleep in that
sleeping bag, when you heard the thud, ran out to find
the mother, your tenant, had jumped out the window,
and was sprawled, bloody, broken in the alley.
It wasn't your fault, but still you lived with her ghost.

# AFTER JOHN SINGER SARGENT'S PAINTING, *ON THE VERANDA*

1

Honey locust leaves
bleached to a silky gold
drift onto the patio, and on
the lean length of him. The
striped lounge chair barely
holds his height. Glasses
off, eyes closed, his long
hands clasped behind his
shaven head, I watch my
husband sleep amidst
cricket trill and wind that
stirs the last of the leaves,
and the scent of pine and
oddly sweet leaf mold.
Mouth relaxed into a half-
smile, he dozes, blanketed
by afternoon sky.

2

You won't always laze in our leather lounger, one foot flat
on the pale carpet, the other resting on your knee—black
socks, black jeans like a 3-D silhouette, veined
hand splayed on the chair arm, bifocals slipping down your

nose, shaved head nodding on the headrest.

I won't always be sitting here on the beige couch
with its ecru flocked flowers, noticing the
roundness of your lids as you read from your
iPad, your long-lobed Buddha ears, those lines
that groove your forehead or the line that incises
your chin. You won't always feel my hand in
yours. I scare myself with winter thoughts.

3

Was it only three months ago that we,
in short sleeves, ate Gino's pizza
at our outdoor table, Citronella flame
flickering on our tomato-sauced
chins, fingers shining with oil,
mozzarella draping from our slices,
the air breathy with hibiscus?

Today a few remaining impatiens bob
in the damp briskness. Molted elm leaves
curl like songless birds, heads tucked
beneath serrated wings. Honey locust
leaves have tattered to ochre lace, dark
pods arched, alien, twisting like hatchlings.

4

How many times have you, like the man in the painting, stretched out your long
legs as you sat on the patio, while I, nearby, read a book or did a crossword?
We didn't talk much. Just breathed the same air and let languid waves of peace
flow between us.
How I wish you were here now. I wouldn't complain about the mosquitos or the
emboldened squirrels. I would just look and look at you.

How could it be that you, all 6'4" of you, walked into St. Francis Hospital for
open-heart surgery and landed in a wheelchair with no bladder or bowel control?
What god punished you? Punished
us? Prometheus was bound to a rock for stealing fire from the gods and giving
it to mortals, but I
am cold, so cold. Wearing a hat and gloves, I shiver in our overheated apartment.

Yesterday, I stood across the street from Little Neck Care Center so that I could
see you in your first-floor window without the obstruction of the overhang. You
were a pale smudge of yourself,
your large hand waving like a ghost hand. How I felt with the autumn leaves
raining down on me,
swirling, and you, inside, no fresh air, no direct sunshine. And because of
Covid, I cannot come near you, cannot touch you. I don't know if I will ever be
able to bring you back to our apartment
with the wide patio where you loved to sit at my side.

# THE HALLELUJAH CHORUS

Like a clarion call to rise, you shot up from your balcony seat and joined in the chorus as if we were not at Lincoln Center, but at a singalong in a barn with a guitar strumming. Even in a barn you, with your croaking bullfrog voice, would only have mouthed the words, you who never even sang in the shower, joined the oratorio as loudly as if you wore a mic. The audience looked up toward the balcony. The oboes, bassoons, trumpets took a breath. The bows on the violins and cellos stalled mid-string. The chorus gave out a rousing *Hal* and then paused before the *luljah*. I tugged hard at your sleeve. With a shake of your head, you woke from your trance, and sat down fast. *Hallelujah.*

# NO CANDLE IS LIT FOR YOU

O, that September Morning when
you strode in for heart surgery and I
believed you'd stride out. The
doctor sporting a bowtie and
ponytail announced the operation
a success, but you no longer had
bowel control and your mind
was pea soup.

The hospital keeps sending me mail—
"Donate to St. Francis Heroes." Do they
mean the nurses and aides who never
came when I rang and rang? Do they
mean the ones who put restraints on
your legs because you set off alarms by
attempting to toilet yourself, those
restraints that you fought against like
Samson trying to hold up the columns
about to fall on him, the restraints
that tore your leg muscles?

How could we have asked for more
when Covid-19 halved the staff,
cut down patients gasping in other
wards? In other words, you were a
victim of history, the Covid-19 era
that is still taking lives and leeched
your chances at life.

Among the virus's victims, you
are a sidebar.

# DO I REALLY LIVE IN NISKAYUNA NOW?

Fat flakes fall on overreaching loblollies, spruce, and scotch pine.
So much sky, a mountain of clouds rent by archipelagos of drizzly gray.
The windows of these large aluminum-sided houses and the occasional
brick are blank.
Sidewalks,
I miss you
as I walk this macadam road, the only honks from geese beating
their way to elsewhere. Oh, MOMA, Carnegie Hall, Times
Square, Soho and Noho, and Frank O'Hara's ghost. Oh, daylight
neon, the Whitney, the pigeons shitting on the Patience and
Fortitude lions in front of the 42nd St. Library.

Oh, my Bernie, partly paralyzed from—
would you believe?—open-heart surgery—I came ahead to ready
this house for you—the ramps, modifications to the bathroom,
the lift, while you wait in Little Neck Care Center. Oh, how you
used to grip my hand as we ran to catch the railroad, you,
with your long strides, always before me. Those lucky days
when conductors forgot to hole-punch our tickets, and we rode
free as hobos.

Come Spring, you will watch me plant a butterfly bush, phlox,
lantana, and blue star. Monarchs, cotton whites,
and pearl crescents will hover about us.
Each morning I will waken to you.

# TABLE FOR TWO

Set for one,
the pour of the dark roast into
the coffee mug with your
photo on it, the heat it brings
to my lips.

Through the window, pine trees hold armfuls of
winter, the winter of you not with me. The pane
reflects my face like a ghostly selfie I can't send you,
the you who will return, not you, the you who will
roll in on a walker,
*rollator,*
it's called, which you keep calling
*Roto-Rooter.*
when you phone from the Home to ask me
to order soap when you mean lotion.

Spring, in the medieval garden, amid oxeyes
and yarrow and unfurling ferns, our laughter
when a monarch landed on your bold nose.

I live between the honk of geese, their shadows fleeing,
between shuddering pixels of night, your wedding ring.

Sixty years ago, in summer, you, a
strapping seventeen, me, fourteen,
on tiptoe when
I kissed you.

Will you still be my lover?
The pines, their armfuls of winter.

# LOOKING OUT THE WINDOW OF OUR HOUSE

The snowbanks are white as fallen clouds
with soft blue-gray shadows. Our rural mailbox
is buried in a froth. The mailman doesn't even
stop. My letters to you pile up in the foyer. Our
rhododendron nearly swallowed in snow still
has a hint of viridian. I've forgotten the names
of the bushes, now pillowy humps on our front
lawn at the house you have not seen.

I think of you turning sideways in your hospital bed
to peer out your second-story window in your
room in Little Neck Care Center.
We often drove past the squat brick building
on our way to elsewhere. In winter, traffic
spewed soot on plowed banks and snow fell
on spindly trees.

I will not call our house home
until you are here with me.

# FIVE MONTHS SINCE I'VE SEEN YOU

Hunched, you roll toward me, red splotches on your hands
that grip the Rollator, your shadow wavering on the faux
gold damask wallpaper.

I stand in the doorway of
room 101
in the Century Hotel where we must stay
until the handicapped bathroom and the lift
are finished in our new home. Your eyes,
damp brown agates above the blue of your
pandemic mask.

This is my husband, whose arms
used to hold me, arms used to lift me.

Sequestered in your room during Covid outbreaks,
sequestered with a mute man who could only blink,
isolated again, again, having to stay three extra weeks
to receive your final vaccine. Once you get the first
in a nursing home, the state will not allow you to get
the follow-up anywhere else.
Then came the snowstorm that kept you longer.
You roll closer with your Rollator.

We cry out each other's names.

# I SEE THE BRUISES BLOOMING ON YOUR BACK

You admit you fell in the garage coming in from a walk.
        I picture you in the half-light, letting go of the handles
of your walker, teetering, then slamming down on the cold concrete,
stunned at the view of the spiderweb ceiling.

        No thought of calling out to me as I called out to you,
searching the winding streets where you, half-blind and deaf with a bum
knee, were not supposed to go alone. I ran up the cul-de-sac,
up Windsor Road
      where cars whizzed, up Alva where drivers pulled out of driveways
   without a glance. My shouts set the crows cawing, set my pulse hammering.

        At your first job, your boss left a trapdoor open. You plunged, breaking
your fall by grabbing the banister. Then you took the creaky flight up,
and went back to work without a word.

What it must have been like for you when I had to kneel to put on your shoes,
bend to zip your jacket, stand on tiptoe to straighten your eyeglasses,
you, who never asked for help, never thought you needed to.

# CAROUSEL OF STARS

As the carousel of stars slowed in my head,
it was the eighteen-year-old you, my future husband,
at my bedside, rubbing my shoulder, squeezing my hand,
urging me, "Stay awake, stay awake."

Blinking, I remembered gym class, the girl next to me,
both hands tight on the grip of her racket
to perfect her tennis swing. Before I could duck,
she swung it with the force of Samson
wielding the jawbone of an ass.

"Why does everything have to happen to you?"
my mother huffed in a haze of Marlboro smoke
as she drove me to St. Joseph's where a nun
x-rayed my head. The doctor who read my x-ray
had a crucifix on his wall. In my daze, I thought I'd
died and was reborn into the wrong religion.

"A concussion," the doctor announced. "She needs
bedrest, but don't let her fall asleep."

My mother dropped me off at our house. "There's
a Yankee Pot Roast dinner in the freezer for you," she said.
"I have to get back to the store. Dad can't be left alone
to answer the phone and work the register."

I only meant to rest, but my eyelids rolled
down like the awning over my father's

storefront window.

When you heard from your kid brother
that I was carried out from the girl's gym
through the boy's on a chair, my head lolling,
you rang and rang my doorbell.

There was no answer, so you drove
to my parents' grocery store, got the housekey,
and wouldn't leave me though your mother
kept phoning. "Come home. This is
her mother's responsibility, not yours."

She was right, but you wouldn't leave me,
and never shamed me with an unkind remark
about her. "I like that she's lively," you often said.

How would I have survived childhood
without you?

# MY HUSBAND'S DEMENTIA

A glass half full, the other half spilled by his
trembling hand.

A clock with an unstoppable cuckoo.
An eraser that cannot stop erasing.

A walker rammed into a parked car.
A midnight call from Joe Biden.

A boat bumping the sides of
a Tunnel of Love.

Moonlight without light.
A star that has no point.

A shaken magic eight-ball— Reply:
hazy, try again.

# FORTUNE

My husband's spine arches like a cat's against the back
of the kitchen chair. Slowly, he takes off his glasses,
rubs his eyes. I watch, held breath as he bobs and lists
in the armless chair, his PB&J sandwich, his sudden
favorite, before him on the table. He won't even take sip of water.
"That guy [his aide] poisons
my water," he claims.

Bernie's stubble is gray on his graying face.
He can't shave, won't let me shave him.
Strings of drool hang from his lower lip.
His mouth caves in as if he's toothless.

When I was 14, in the darkened penny arcade,
I put a nickel in the slot of the fortuneteller's booth.
The lights switched on. The wooden lady with the
cracked face and faded satin dress, a collar of
yellowed lace, jerked to life.

"Will I marry Bernie?" I asked.

Her jointed wooden hand made a twitching arc over
a tarot spread. Her head moved back and forth
before she slid her answer through the slot.

"A smile is worth a thousand frowns," her card had said.

# BERRY-PICKING

I watch my husband rip apart a bag of frozen blueberries that
roll into the freezer bin, and onto the floor, his slippered feet
squashing them—splotches of berry juice on the tiled floor
and in the grout. Like the blood my father saw running between
the cobblestones of his city with the statue of the Tsar.

My husband spent five months in a "care facility" where he was
allotted invalid portions. My food packages disappeared. I
couldn't visit because of Covid. Like Romeo, I stood on the
sidewalk waving up at him in his second-story window,
his face, wraithlike.

"Don't bring him home," doctors warned.
"He's a fall risk, addled, helpless. He could set a fire."

He taught himself to walk again with a rolling walker,
but he forgets the word scissors or what he did a moment ago.
What he doesn't forget is hunger that stays on his skin like a blue tattoo.

Now I berry-pick in our kitchen, whisking berries from the dark
beneath the fridge with a yardstick. While I mop every drop of berry blood,
I miss my husband as he was when we knelt, thigh to thigh in the
strawberry patch, pushing aside the crowns of tooth-edged leaves
with their silky under-hairs to reach close to the roots, twisting
the stems gently to get the berries off.

# DOWNPOUR AND THUNDER

I write in my bedroom with a combo lock on the
outside knob that my husband can't figure out, no
matter how close behind me he stands to watch me key
in the four numbers. My house is 24/7 inhabited by
aides, male aides—my husband threatened a female
aide with scissors to her neck.

Last night a female had to fill in for the male aide
who got a heart attack. While I was sequestered in my
locked room with a rain and thunder app playing
loudly (sounding like 1,000 flushing toilets and
something vaguely gastric for thunder) I heard
a scuffle. Like a merwoman in an aquatic tank,

I swam toward my door, palms groping the wood which
became a pane of glass, but my body stayed in bed. This
morning, when I turned off the storm, my husband was
gone. I learned he'd slapped and kicked the female aide
who called for help. They took him away to an address
unknown to me, and I don't want to ask.

Once my husband had leaped in front of me when a car
was about to jump the sidewalk. He had pushed
our car up an icy hill when it stalled with me inside
so I wouldn't get cold, wouldn't get wet.

I am writing with my door open, sunlight from the tall windows
pouring into the hallway where I can walk with loud footsteps.
I write to keep my door open.

# COUNTRY LIFE

Buying this ample ranch house in the country, I
dreamed I could rescue you, my husband, from the
nursing home where I couldn't visit you
because of Covid, where you were starved,
quarantined in your room. Who knew that apart
from the stroke caused by open-heart surgery,
you would be diagnosed with Lewy body dementia,
which creates delusions, paranoia? Who could guess
that all the knives and scissors would have to be hidden,
that all the doors would require inside and outside locks
so you can't escape to beat up the old fellow across the
street who you are convinced is an enemy?

I pictured us sitting on the patio, side by side, my
hand on yours as we looked out at our garden of
flowers mentioned by Shakespeare—columbine,
chamomile, cowslip, daffodils, larkspur, poppy.
How I roared at Stratford-upon-Avon when you,
with your fat, bee-stung lip, slurred— *Haply I*
*think on thee, and then my state,*
   *(Like to the lark at break of day arising*
*From sullen earth) sings hymns at heaven's gate,*
then you whistled a spluttering jumble of notes
that made me open my umbrella.

Now, sitting beside me on the patio, you jam my chair
against the house, jarring my arm, trying to get closer.
Who knew my dreams would be broken by you in the

hallway, lunging your body against the front door,
bellowing, "Let me in, Let me in."

# PASTORAL

My love, your hearing aids amp all sound— my
words lost to you in the honk of geese, the sough of
wind tossing the trees. I hold onto the backrest bar
of your walker. The vibrations from its wheels on
cracked macadam travel up my arm like the tremble
I felt the first time we touched.

# I WANT TO WRITE A POEM

I will not let this poem reveal
the long scar, still red and raised
on my husband's chest, surrounded
by graying curls, nor
his ropy arms blooming with blood.

I want to write a poem about him running
ahead of me on the beach, the green kite
we bought at Woolworths bobbing in the cloudless sky
and me chasing after him, laughing,
a poem that notes his size
fourteen footprints in the sand,
and shows him spinning to face me, running
backward lithely like a winged god.

I will not let this poem
reveal his trembling right hand nor
the lid-droop of his left eye
nor smell the sourness
of medication in his sweat, nor hear the chirp
and buzz of his hearing aids.

I want to write a poem about him
holding our newborn daughter in the palm
of his hand, and pacing with our colicky son,
patting his back, my son's face rising
above my husband's shoulder
like a pocket mirror of him.

I will not let this poem reveal
my husband leaning as he walks
as if he's a pine tree in a forest reaching
toward light, nor the whisper
of his Velcro-closing slippers
on the vined carpet, nor allow this poem
to show him opening the door in the middle
of the night to accept a delivery from Amazon,
his hands holding only air.

# MARTY

Wind howls and shrieks like storybooks say.
The neighbor's German Shepherd ululates each
night of my first country winter, my first
without you in fifty-four years.

Each time you phone from the nursing home,
I hear that same old woman in the background
singing the same off-key song from the sticky
rachet of her throat.

*Don't repeat yourself,* I beg when you tell me, over and
over: *Marty has been my best friend since high school
and we both married Rockaway girls the very same year.*

I know. I knew you since high school. I
went to Marty's wedding with you. We
danced to their wedding song— *The
First Time Ever I Saw Your Face.*

You were so tall then, your dark curls thick.
The wind has lost its breath. The
neighbor's Shepherd skulks
around his rimed yard.

# LEWY BODY DEMENTIA

There's a monsoon here in Ulster County jeweling
the iron deck with tears, erasing the Catskill Mountains
from the picture window, graying the sky, keeping me
from the garden with its puff of bridal hydrangeas,
Gladiator Allium— those purple globes sending forth a
sweet oniony scent, pompom China asters, and fat
toads that kerplop across the path.

I hope as my husband sits on the couch, my
arm around him, the incessant sizzle of rain
will calm him.

His eyelids droop, then close, but he bolts up, knocks
over his walker.

"This place is bugged," he insists, squeezing my arm so
tight I know I'll have yet another bruise.

This afternoon, on our fifty-fourth wedding anniversary,
our daughter had to call Daughters of Sarah Nursing Home,
Kingsway Arms, Capital Care, anywhere he will be safe,
and I will be safe from him.
This will be his second nursing home.

Damn Lewy Body Dementia that makes him
write secret codes on my t-shirts, spit out and stamp
on his tranquilizers, believe I am poisoning him,
push past me out the door to the road
where he isn't supposed to go alone.

# WHERE HE LIVES

I blink at the windshield,
hardly believing my eyes created
the squashed mosquito splatter
even though I know
my maculae are collapsing.
I ride beside my son in silence
toward the Home
where my husband now lives.

When we arrive, my husband
rises on shaky legs and toddles
into our son's arms just as our son
once toddled into his.
Our son presents his father
with chocolate chip cookies
baked by his oldest boy
from my husband's mother's recipe.
My husband's stubbled face, stiff
these days, breaks into a wide smile.

I sense the small boy
in him, the boy in his Wavecrest
apartment: air of schnitzel,
                    of bratwurst,
                        of Käsespatzle,
and his parakeet,
Mickey, bobbing, bobbing
on his shoulder, chirping,

cheeping, lightening
the heavy refugee air.

# NO ONE

Even with the dwindling gray matter of dementia, you
croon with each spoonful of Spaghetti-O's
that make it to your mouth. No one wanted to live as much

as your namesake, Uncle Bernard who survived Auschwitz,
Uncle Bernard whose kidney was removed, no anesthesia,
by Dr. Mengeles, and injected with parasites.

Had I been in a Camp, I would have vaulted myself against
the electrified barbed wire fence to stop the stench of human ash,
to become human ash. Your father, at ninety, incontinent,

half-blind, sat in his father's mahogany armchair
secreted out of Berlin, looking out over the artificial lake
of his assisted living center with its fountain, watching mallards

and Canadian geese paddle in the mist, and sighed
with the contentment of having eaten
a thick slice of cherry kuchen.

No one wants to survive more than you.

# SELFIE

Imagine all the likes I'd get if I posted this
seated selfie of me and my husband, me leaning
into him, him with his hand on my shoulder,
our smiles. They don't have to know the couch
we're on is in a nursing home. They don't have
to see the wheelchair waiting to receive him,
nor do they need to know a thing about the
catheter he must wear.
All I will show them is this moment:
                    our faces kissed by window light,
                    the Japanese maple burning scarlet
                    before leaf fall.

# TOODLING

"Toodling," they call it, my husband propelling
his wheelchair with his slippered feet down the
hallway of the Kingsway Arms.

He looks empowered, head held high,
shoulders back like King Tut on a rolling throne,
stopping to nod at this one / that one, toodling to
the nurse's station to grab a banana or a pack of
chocolate chip cookies from the basket.

How lovely to find him out of his narrow room,
and in the communal one with its fireplace, giant wall
TV, and the view of snow-covered pines and icicles.

My husband, who wrestled a knife-wielding thief
to the sidewalk, who went into the projects ruled by
the Crips and Bloods to deliver medicine to his
customers, has not lost his spunk. The nursing home
aides have had to put alarms on his bed, his mat, his
wheelchair, and a bracelet alarm on his wrist
to stop him from escaping.

He fights to get four chocolate Ensures
instead of one. "That many," the dietician tells him,
"will build up too much calcium and Vitamin A in
your system." He tightens his fists, shoots eye-
arrows at her.

Let him fight. Let him escape what waits.

# THE OTHER SIDE

Remember when we, holding hands,
walked the lone path at the arboretum,
and suddenly two full-grown deer
leaped over us like a moving arch?
We saw their underbellies, held our breath
until they landed on the other side.

# ROOM 328

When I run my fingers over your stubbly face, your
corded neck, you toss your head lightly on your
pillow, make that low growl I know so well. I won't
sit in the visitor's chair. I stand, leaning toward you
to take you in. You give me that come-hither look.

I feel a flutter in my womb. I feel my blood
heat up. If your nursing home bed weren't
so narrow, I'd lie down beside you, press
my body against yours, never mind that
you are all bones now like your uncle, your
namesake when he was liberated
from Auschwitz.

I hear the aides' carts rattling in the
hall. Any moment someone will come
through the door to feed or change
you, give you meds.

It's like when the kids were small and
we parked them in front of the TV
to slip into our room, breathless.
Now I kiss your lips hard.
Your tremoring hand reaches for me.
The door opens.

# PHILOMEN AND BAUCIS

Milkweed twirled around us like sprites in feathery tutus. Gently
squeezed, snapdragons opened their mouths like baby birds for
worms, or when, decades before, we tickled the cheeks
of our infants so they'd root for the nipple.

Standing beneath the embrace of a willow,
I told you the myth of Philemon and Baucis, the old couple
who, gracious to gods disguised as beggars, were granted
their wish—to die at the same moment
and be turned into trees.

You in your straw hat, me in my long floral dress and
parasol must have looked like a Victorian couple.
A woman asked to take our picture.

Then your left hand began to tremor, your face to
stiffen. "Smile," I'd beg.

Looking at that photo on your wall in the
nursing home where you're bedridden, I feel
you walking next to me with your long
strides, your wide smile. You lead me past
jewelweed, rhododendron, the perfect
geometry of mountain laurel.

# LETHE

Someday he will forget my name. my face
But not today, please
Not today.

"Do you know me?" I ask,
Taking his hand.
"Do you love me?"

His mouth opens to no sound.
Out the window, the naked tree
Makes an arthritic appeal to the sky.

# GONE, BUT NOT

You, shivering in bed in your overheated room,
bedsores suppurating, each like a lava maw
eating your flesh, each a ridged raw mountain,
each day more on your heels, your hips, the
hunger they have for your skin like the hunger
I have for you to rise like Lazarus, and me
once again having to double-step to keep up.

Each visit, I busy myself going to
the fridge down the hall to bring
you thickened orange juice that I
hold for you as you sip through a
bent straw.

"You can ring for me," the nurse says.
"I'll bring whatever he needs."

I don't tell her I'm scared to make
too many demands when I must
leave you in the hands of strangers
while your flesh is eaten away, and
you're still here, but not.

# WINTER CAN GO NOW

My husband can no longer chew and breathe
at the same time. Thickened liquid
is his sustenance so he won't choke. Winter

can go now. As the aide massages
his cheeks to help him swallow,
I watch his wall TV where bombs
fall on a Ukrainian village. There's a report
of Ukrainian children dying of dehydration.
My husband is hydrated through a bent straw
held to his parched lips as he sips
thickened liquid. In the clean filth

of the Nursing Home, my husband
has a bed and is nursed and cozened
while orphaned children
cross the border alone.
How blessed my husband is dying
in a bed beneath an unbombed sky.

My relatives in Babi yar,
in Berdychiv, and my husband's
in Auschwitz, were stacked
body on body, thrown or fallen
with a soft thud of flesh on flesh
or the crack of bone on bone.

Each day an aide shaves my husband's

face. Each day Ukrainians huddle in subway
stations. Each day is worse than the last.

Shoes piled in the Holocaust Museum,
shoes in the rubble of the Towers,
empty shoes on the snowy streets
of the Ukraine. Winter
can go now. Persephone

can be raised from her tomb. How
can we mourn come morning?

# WHAT HAPPENED TO US

In the marshland, phragmites overtake the habitat
like age overtakes us. No more long drives or any
at all with both of us nearly purblind. No more
dashes to catch the LIRR bound for the Met or the
MOMA. How we laughed when I spent twenty
minutes studying what I thought was a wall
sculpture at P.S. 1. It turned out to be a thermostat.
I can still smell the tangy carrot ginger soup
we spooned in their café.

# ONE PIE, HURRY PLEASE

I want you, in your nursing
home bed no longer able to
breathe while you chew,
sustained on thickened liquid,
I want you to smell bubbling
tomato sauce topped with
mozzarella on a thick crust slid
out of a woodburning oven
with a long-handled spatula.

I know when I say *lemon*, my
mouth waters. *Anchovy*, my nose
crinkles. Let me awaken your
taste buds: *oregano, hot peppers,*
*pepperoni.*

Let yourself feel strings of cheese
stretch from your teeth to the
slice. Let yourself grin as you did
when we leaned in to taste each
other's garlic breath.

# HOSPICE

You are in a cranked-up bed or in a reclining
wheelchair, mouth ajar, lips and tongue cracked.
You can no longer press the help button
to alert an aide.

I lift the cup to your peeling lips.
This, and my hand on your forehead, on your shaven scalp,
stubbled face, are the ways you know my love.

Your limbs, crooked from disuse, make you
look like a spider, but your eyes, those brown,
long-lashed pools, still look at me like no man
ever will again, look at me with the memory
of my taste, my scent, my throaty cry.

Your voice is low from weakness.
I'm surprised I can feel the vibration of your words in
your ropy arm that I realize I'm holding tightly. I
bring a glass of thickened water to your parched lips.

# FAILED PANTOUM

*(lines sung by the Righteous Brothers, 1965)*

It cannot be a cherub who comes for him.
He needs a muscular William Blake angel, powerful, strapping.
I see my husband as he was—sinewy, long-limbed.
His eyes are dimmed, but I remember how he once beheld me.

A Blake-like angel must come for him, not ethereal, but strapping.
Terrifying and beautiful like the angels Rilke called out to. Each
Visit, I sing the song to him we used to slow-dance to.

My husband is now terrifying, but beautiful as the angels Rilke called out to.
*O, my love, my darling, I've hungered for your touch.*
Do you hear me sing the song we used to slow-dance to?
*Time goes by so slowly and time can do so much.*

His dying goes so slowly that he is cold to the touch.
My husband's hands tremble, but *I hunger for his touch.*
No cherub can lift my love from this railed bed.
Blake's angel, come, come for him.

# YOU OPEN YOUR EYES

Just as I walk in, as if you've sensed
my footsteps in the long hallway of
your sleep. Your hands are gauzed
like winter frost, fingers so cold.

Soon you will not have to lie in the bed
in this small room, nor have to be coffined
and buried. A burst of flame, heat at last,
and you will be ash, ash that I will,
as you wished, sprinkle on the beach
where we met.

There will be no weeds to pull, no stones
to lay on a grave, no words inscribed on
a headstone, just sand beneath your feet
again and the sea pulling you
into its foamy embrace.

# SLEEP APP

The wind's whip, whoosh, the rain's ratatat,
and the soft crackle of thunder lull my lids
shut, but I fret about you, my husband
in your bed at the Kingsway Arms,
still unsure of how to press the *Help Me*
gizmo,
and me, alone
in this house meant for us.
*Who will hold me*
*when I hear my dead mother howl*
*from her railed bed at Pilgrim State?*
*Who will hold me when I cry out,*
*"No, Daddy, no!"*

Without you beside me, I pop in and out of dreams like a cuckoo
in a clock. I, a graying troubadour,
sing a lullaby of missing things:
shopping lists, passwords, keys, scissors, the deed...

You were my compass's
fixed foot. Nothing is fixed now.
Once I had a landline.
These days I have two cell phones.
I use one
to find the other.

# SHE DIDN'T TELL HIM SHE WAS COMING

A hundred unchanged diapers, the mélange of fungus feet,
the whine of anonymous farts follows her to room 328 where
her husband, in his wheelchair, waits.

She didn't tell him when she was coming, or even
that she was, but he waits, like she waits to see
him, and seeing him, she can't wait until he's
dead. (There, she's said it.)

But that night, the cork pops off the bottle
of Merlot in a high cabinet she can't
reach without him, can't uncork without
him, yet she pours a glass for him, for
her. When he tips his head back to drink,
she watches his Adam's Apple bob,
senses his contented sigh
like breath in her ear.

She runs her hands down his corded neck,
his bony shoulders, down his long arms,
the skin like bark. He holds her to him.
They kiss, his lips moist, not with drool, but wine-slicked.

The next day, she will double-pace
toward room 328. Death,
please wait.

# THE CALL

1.

Night lurks at the edge of day like a
cataract not ripe enough for surgery,
like the black velvet background
of a paint-by-numbers clown.

Night rubs its fur against you like a
witch's familiar and sweeps through
your home like an impending phone
call announcing someone's end that
you know is coming, but still, night
seeps into your psyche, keening an
urgent dirge.

Night is your first blanket, cloaking
the cream on your newborn skin.
Night is your last blanket, your
shroud. Night is a phone ringing in
the day or in the dark.

2.

I know the hour will come
when I get the call
that you have left life,

but it will not feel like an hour.

It will be a moment
in what had been our lives
together and now only mine
with a trove of moments
that toll and toll.

The hours stopper our tear ducts,
make us long in the tooth,
but you, you
will always be my youth.

Even now when your tongue
is too stiff to speak, I see life
in your eyes, brown and beseeching.

3.

A black cat pads out of a driveway toward me
as I plod in the sauna of August heat
in a place where I've only recently landed.

Up the street, a crow lands on the black asphalt.
Neighbors peer at me through their car windows.
How can they know that my husband is dying?
How can they know I'm being chased
by my grandmother's omens told to me
in the dark of my childhood?

Just before I get the call that my husband has died,
a hawk screeches and screeches from a treetop.

4.

All those months of sequestering, and still
Covid came for you, made your lungs creaky
bellows. I would have had to wear a paper
gown, heavy mask, a visor, latex gloves to be
with you. How could I touch your skin? How
could I speak to you with my words
like mist on a window?

I set up your iPad and mine
to keep watch over you.

The hospice nurse said I was keeping you alive.
How could that be when you couldn't hear?
Couldn't see?
I let my screen go dark.
Ten minutes later, I got the call

that you were dead.

# VENOM

A black fly lands on the knuckle of my pointer finger,
stings me before I can swat it off. I am allergic
to the fly's venom. Remember

that summer in Cape Cod? No fly landed on you,
I got a bite that swelled like purple.
dough and burned, and would not heal
even with saltwater soaks or Calamine.

The only doctor we could find open on a Saturday
was a pediatrician. At twenty, I looked so young
he gave me a lollypop. How we laughed!
And now my knuckle is swelling with black fly venom,
and you are not here to turn it into a crackpot adventure.
Anything is a molehill compared to the loss of you.

# HOW YOU LOVED AUTUMN

The thin braided fronds of the Chinese Silver Grass crinkle
as they rub together in wind.
The burning bush goes neon against the pines.
You can prick your finger on the tips of maple leaves.

Shadows are blue/violet upside-down twins of trees.
How strange the veined quivering aspen leaves don't quiver in wind.
After you raked the sloped lawn for an hour, you jumped in the pile
        with the children.
Today the maple leaves are eaten to lace.

# DEAR BERNIE,

A silhouette of a long-legged guy, arms
swinging at his sides, came toward me
today. I knew it wasn't you. I knew it
wasn't flesh, but I still hurried toward the
shadow of you, past a guard dog grr-ing in a
yard, past the ranch house with the lending
library on the lawn and the twin Adirondack
chairs on the porch, past the blue plastic
sheath of a New York Times blowing in the
gutter along with the fallen leaves. As if I
were bunion-less, knees not cracking, I ran
toward the you I knew was not you.

# HAD YOU WRITTEN ME LOVE LETTERS

I would not have been able to make out your spiky sprawl,
but letters weren't needed. We only lived blocks away
before living together.

During the Vietnam War, you manned the pharmacy
of a city hospital where the parking lot was target
practice for zip guns and Glocks.
They never found out who added acid
to the antibiotic ointment. You were so worried
for patients that you committed to nights
and weekend shifts no one else would take.

I was the one who quaked as you recounted
all of this in a steeled voice. Life
let you come home to me
until life left. I wish I had letters
from you whether I could make them
out or not.

# WHEREVER I AM, I WAKE UP IN FAR ROCKAWAY

Even in Phoenix, I wake to the sough of the sea,
its salt breath like ghost messages. I wake to my
father's footprints in snow that led away from the
house to his grocery each dawn. In the yellow
kitchen beneath the Felix-the-Cat wall clock,
my mother squeezes fresh orange juice and serves
my two sisters and me soft-boiled eggs
in tiny rose petal eggcups.

Wherever I am, I wake to my husband as he was
at seventeen, his arm around my waist, his foot
resting on the metal rail of the boardwalk as we
watch the Wednesday night fireworks.

The gulls cry. Everyone is alive.
Footprints are fresh in the snow.

# WEDDING SILHOUETTE

Six months after you died, I posted the silhouette on Facebook.
I, a bride of 19, you, a groom of 22 in sepia,
leaning into each other
for a kiss.

"I miss him," I wrote. "I miss him."
Within a day, 83 friends responded with "GIFs":
teddy bears bearing hearts
Charley Brown's arms open for hugs
a tearful puppy holding a rose
It was as if the viral world were our wedding guests.

But as the like, love, care, and tears emojis thinned,
I felt as if I had just gotten the call, "Your husband is dead."
I will never post about us again.

# HIS SHOES

From the floor of the closet, I pick up his shoes,
cradle each to my chest as if they are children I'm
about to give up for adoption before putting then
in a bag for charity. The innersoles
are dark with mourning, laces languid, size 14 black wingtips
that made him look like an undercover cop,
Adidas he scrubbed with a mix of baking soda and vinegar,
work boots Van Gogh might have painted.

A walking man, my husband. After 14 hours
of work, he'd drive 19 miles to Brighton
Beach to stroll miles in the salt air, watch
slivers of moon rock on the sea, hear gulls,
inhale the aromas of pierogi and borscht
wafting from Tatiana's, slip five bucks
to the bony-shouldered old man
serenading diners on his accordion.

Winters, or when it rained, he tracked miles
around Cinnabon-scented malls. When he could buy
shoes there at a discount he did—piles of sneakers
stiff and shiny, rainboots that buckled,
rainboots you drew on over other shoes, loafers
that he stuck pennies in, moccasins.

"Stop!" I'd insist.

I didn't know this was how he'd listen.

# TODAY I PROMISED

Will be the last time
I button myself into your long, black
winter coat, the wool soft as a whisper,
sleeves falling almost to my knees, hem
circling me on the blonde wooden floor.

This is how it was to be with you,
my straight-backed man, a full
foot taller than me, my hand
gloved in yours.

I would keep the coat always,
but winter is coming
for the hungry, the cold,
those who I know you'd open
your arms to. This coat

empty of you, that no longer holds
your woodsy scent, can still
embrace, give warmth.

# DINING ROOM TABLE

Hewn from trees felled in Idaho,
grain smoothed by years of Thanksgivings,
seders, squabbles, and elbows,
now all without you. Our grieving
circles like a dark halo.
The empty space like a leaf
taken from the tree of life. Widowed,
I set out plates for the living,
my voice mournful, cello-like.
When I see your face in our children,
their children, it's like you
not felled, but still growing, living

somewhere outside and inside me.

# PANDEMONIUM

You brought home a small, white carton
with a wire handle, the type you expect to hold
Chinese takeout. A green parakeet flew out
and beat its wings around our apartment, tail
feathers fanning, legs tucked against its breast
like airplane wheels after takeoff.

You dubbed the bird Prince Albert
because of its golden crown. I could not
shoo the bird from our lives, not when I knew
the chirps of parakeets had brightened the rooms
of your refugee childhood.

I loved the sparrows that tittered on our sill, the terns
and gulls that dipped and surged in the salt air of our
seaside town, their haunting cries, but not a bird
indoors, skirting lamps, bumping into the slats
of blinds, the dubious blur of a bird.

I screamed when Albert landed on my head. Even
with my wild thicket hair, I felt his talons
on my scalp. Albert, panicked, tried to fly off,
but my hair, wound in his claws, lassoed him back.

"Shh, you're scaring him," you said, making
kissing sounds, not to me, but to Albert.

Soon, the way Albert chirped when he heard you coming

down the hall, the way he sat on your shoulder, head-
bobbing, chirping bird-talk into your ear, eating a diced
apple from your big palm, my heart was lassoed.

A pandemonium of parakeets should serenade
your passage into the ethers.

# WHAT COUNTS AS A PROPER GOODBYE

My hands on the smooth rosewood of your funerary box.
Inside, the gist of your body, the grains and atoms of you.
I keep the box on a closed shelf in our / now my bedroom
I couldn't have borne burying you somewhere out there,
miles from me, among strangers. We are no strangers

to ashes, so many relatives ended that way in the camps. My
grandfather's cousin, my namesake, arrested in France. Your
Opa's cousin, Willi, shell-shocked in WWI,
fighting for the Fatherland.

How many reasons must I summon to have you near me?
I could not put you in the ground for the work of worms.

# NAMING

White snakeroot, blue wood aster, shrubby cinquefoil,
names that would be unknown to me without my
PictureThis app. Snap a pic and slowly a green haze
glides down as the app processes your request, then
gives you a clear picture with the name of the plant
that you can file in your mind and call forth,
even as winter blankets the earth,
and grief's forked tongue hisses,
"You are alone. You are alone."

# WAKING

Slip into your arms, your legs, remember your
name, but do not go into the story of your pain
like eating a slice of arsenic cake.

Open to morning without mourning. The crows
already have a lot to say, barking from the linden tree,
shaking its heart-shaped leaves.

The doves coo an aubade. The deck pings with
the droplets of last night's rain.
Some sequin drops cling to the windows.

The world will not let you stay in the dank of
sorrow. Raise your eyes to the cloudbanks.
Light will silver the edges and the breeze
will puff the clouds past.

# THE FAUX WIDOW

"Are you alone?" people ask.
"I used to be," I say. I don't tell
them that everyday this summer,
a blue jay has lit on the
loosestrife, the hydrangea, the
porch rail.

What company is a blue jay they
would wonder and likely think *this*
*woman has birdseed for brains.*

"Are you alone?" my next-door neighbor asks,
in English peppered with Cantonese. I nod
instead of telling her "Not while the Rose of
Sharon still blooms at the edge of my yard."

I must pretend I no longer have a husband
even though we are together on the winding
streets. Together we see the purple balloon
flowers, the white clusters of mock
vervains, and the blue jay. Here he is again.

# ROLODEX

Before computers, with two fingers
you typed each card with your customers' names,
dates of birth, addresses, phone numbers,
and their prescribed medications
including all their doctors' contact info
which made, in my estimation, your little pharmacy
the best in all of Brooklyn.

Flipping through the yellowed cards of my old Rolodex,
I find Paradise Salon, a beauty parlor I no longer need
since Alopecia stole my hair, names of friends I lost
to war, politics, or cancer, and the phone number
and address of Shelbourne Chemists.

Can I still buy refills for this card catalogue?
Rolodexes went out with the corded dial phone
I used to run to answer in my teens, hoping it was you.

# THE GARDENER RODE HIS MOWER OVER THE DRAINPIPES

Now their ends are sealed mouths that must be pried open.
What tool do I use to make drainpipes speak water again
and what will they say with their ripples,
gurgles, gushes,
eddies,
and drips?

Rain pings the eaves and makes each grass blade shake,
and the rhododendron, not in flower yet, stay close to the ground.

How restless you would be on a day like this,
with cloud cover covering the sun.
I can still see you shifting from one leg
to another at the window,
you as tall as the tall windows.

I am just beginning to pinken
like the coleus leaves
and bloom like the red-orange petals
of the Flaming Katy in the pot
on our kitchen table where we used to eat.

I hear you call my name.
I smell your piney scent.

# ABOUT THE AUTHOR

**Rochelle Jewel Shapiro**'s novel, Miriam the Medium (Simon & Schuster, 2005), was nominated for the Harold U. Ribelow Award. She's published essays in NYT (Lives) and Newsweek. Her poetry, short stories, and essays have appeared or are forthcoming in many literary magazines such as La Presa, Mudlark, Neologism Poetry Journal, Packingtown Review, The Iowa Review, The Doctor T.J. Eckleburg Review, Stone Path Review, Frontier Poetry, Santa Fe Literary Review, Stand, Carbon Culture Review, Cider Press Review, Cutbank Literary Journal, Edison Literary Review, Euphony Journal, Inkwell Magazine, Amarillo Bay, Bayou Magazine, Poet Lore, Crack the Spine, Compass Rose, Controlled Burn, Cumberland River Review, The Furious Gazelle, Glint Literary Journal, The Griffin, Grub Street, Los Angeles Review, Reunion: The Dallas Review, East Jasmine Review, Litbreak Magazine, The Virginia Normal, Chantwood Magazine, The MacGuffin, Memoir And, Moment, The Moth, Rougarou, Negative Capability, Penumbra, The Louisville Review, Amoskeag, Organs of Vision and Speech Magazine, Pennsylvania English, Entropy Magazine, Rio Grande Review, riverSedge, Rogue Agent, Seven CirclePress: A Literary Micropress, Sierra Nevada Review, Steam Ticket, Streetlight Magazine, Swamp Ape Review, Licking River Review, Whistling Shade, Peregrine, Gulf Coast, Existere, Passager, Midway Journal, Moria Literary Magazine, Empty Mirror, Sanskrit Magazine, Typishly, Underwood Press, and Willow Review.

Her poetry has been nominated twice for the Pushcart Prize, and won the Branden Memorial Literary Award from Negative Capability. Spry Magazine nominated her poem for the Best of the Net.

She currently teaches writing at UCLA Extension.
Find Her At: https://rochellejshapiro.com On twitter: @rjshapiro

# ACKNOWLEDGMENTS

Grateful acknowledgements are made to the following journals, where versions of these poems have appeared:

"Wedding Album, 1967," —Sweet: A Literary Confection

"I Love You Like German Black Forest Cake" — Evening Street Review

"Country Life" —Open Arts Forum

"When No One Is Near Us" —Brushfire

"Murmur" —Typehouse

"May I Ask Your Name," "Marty," "Table for Two," "Five Months Since I've Seen You" —Flights

"Do I Really Live in Niskayuna Now" —Hey, I'm Alive

"Berry-Picking" —Apricity

"Philomen and Baucis" —A Thin Slice of Anxiety

"One Pie, Hurry Please" —St. katherine's Review

"She Didn't Tell Him She Was Coming," "Winter Can Go Now," —Mudfish

## PRAISE FOR *DEATH, PLEASE WAIT*

From the radiant sparks of a teenaged courtship to the immeasurable pleasures of a long, deeply felt marriage, to the shock of separation-by-grave-illness, Shapiro's poems about her life with her beloved Bernie flow like the most immersive novel, unfolding the story of a soul-mated relationship in language so gorgeous, it stops your breath even as it opens your heart. How lucky, lucky, these two lovers were. And how lucky, lucky we readers are to experience their journey.

**Caroline Leavitt, New York Times bestselling author of 13 *novels, including Pictures of You* and *With Or Without You***

These are poems of intense feelings and exactness. To say they are grief poems is only to recognize their beauty, love, generosity, and longing. Death, Please Wait, boldly sings of our mutable world, where each of us wakes into something frighteningly new.

**June Gould, Ph. D.**
**Author of *Winter in All of Us, E.P. Dutton.***

June Gould is a master workshop leader for the International Women's Writing Guild and is a poet, novelist, and memoirist.

## PRAISE FOR *DEATH, PLEASE WAIT*

*Death, Please Wait*, by Rochelle Shapiro is a poignant, agonizing, elegiac celebration of her husband's battle with dementia. These poems are extraordinary investigations of a heart breaking in the face of loss. Shapiro has managed, with great care, affection, anger, and love, to show us her experience taking care of her Bernie. The astounding nature of these poems is that there is so much feeling—pure feeling—in them. These are not sentimental poems. They are historical and personal and beautifully crafted. Mostly, they plead for the process of dying to slow down. For death to hold up and wait a second. When you read these poems, you want to throw a lasso around death, dying process, and hold it back because you know it's coming, and you want to stop it, you want to life to be victorious. You want to put your arms around the speaker and stay with her awhile. Of course, you can't do that. What you can do is hold this book for a long time and let it breathe life into the small corners of your day. *Death, Please Wait* is not something to wait on. It has that much lifeblood in its pages.

**Matthew Lippman**
**Author of *Mesmerizingly Sadly Beautiful***

## PRAISE FOR *DEATH, PLEASE WAIT*

*Death, Please Wait* heaves with love and bone-crushing loss and traverses the agonizing terrain of the death of Shapiro's husband. I was only two poems in, when, 'You rock me in your long arms like the boat moored / on the black river that I will board and row to you', ended me. Not since Sharon Old's' *Stag's Leap* have I been so devastated nor so profoundly moved. In these tender-yet-earth-shattering poems, Shapiro peels layers from the inside lining of her heart and somehow warms us in its aching chambers. She takes grief apart and somehow puts us all back together again. In poems where the bed is a country, a landscape of soft snores and the naked tree makes an arthritic appeal to the sky, these almost-hymns are conversations between us, the living, and our own not-yet-dead. They are reminders, *as snow falls*, to truly live, *in this the winter of our lives*. Read them to feel alive.

**Ali whitelock,**
**Author of *The lactic acid in the calves of your despair***

## PRAISE FOR *DEATH, PLEASE WAIT*

*Death, Please Wait* is a collection of brutally honest poems about the death of one's true and lifelong love. As we read, a picture slowly forms of Bernie, a 6'4" fierce-eyed man marked by the Holocaust, a fighter, a pharmacist, a man cared for in illness by his adoring wife who endures his bedridden state, his limbs thinned, with great devotion. The poems, all beautifully rendered with details of a foregone New York City world and incredible realism, follow an arc that mirrors the path of many mourners — from only remembering your loved one in illness, to promise and possibility from immense gratitude for the love they experienced. Shapiro will forever hear Bernie's voice saying I love you in her ear, and forever remember his desire for his wife to go on.  Poem after poem, from memories of pharmacies and cutting pills, to a shoe collection and his oversized coat, to a Yankees game and a Johnny Mathis concert, to the horrors of aging and a non-working hearing aide, to inhuman details of nursing homes, hospital rooms, and finally hospice are testaments to true love as well as the power of healing as this couple are still bound forever *on the winding streets*.

**Paul Schaeffer,**
**Author of *The Cruelties of Brooklyn***

## MUDFISH INDIVIDUAL POET SERIES

#1 *Dementia Pugilistica*, David Lawrence

#2 *black diaries*, Jill Hoffman

#3 *Too Too Flesh*, Doug Dorph

#4 *Skunk Cabbage*, Harry Waitzman

#5 *Husk*, Terry Phelan

#6 *marbles*, Mary du Passage

#7 *Fires in Sonoma*, Terry Phelan

#8 *Rending the Garment*, Willa Schneberg

#9 *Vilnius Diary*, Anna Halberstadt

#10 *Single Woman*, Dell Lemmon

#11 *The Gates of Pearl*, Jill Hoffman

#12 *Notes for a Love Poem*, Mary du Passage

#13 *Conversations with the Horizon*, E.J. Evans

# 14 *Are You Somebody I Should Know?*, Dell Lemmon

#15 *Losing It*, Richard Fein

#16 *Mad Love*, Terry Phelan

#17 *The Cruelties of Brooklyn*, Paul Schaeffer

#18 *Dear Yiddish*, Richard Fein

#19 *Death, Please Wait*, Rochelle Jewel Shapiro

MUDFISH FICTION SERIES

#1 *Stoned,* Jill Hoffman

Coming soon:

# 2 *Arnold 2,* Robert Steward

All Mudfish titles available from www.Mudfish.org

Box Turtle Press, Inc.
184 Franklin Street
New York, NY 10013